Looking Back at
Houses and Homes

EDITORIAL PLANNING
AMR

M
MACMILLAN

First published 1988

Published by
MACMILLAN EDUCATION LTD
Houndmills, Basingstoke, Hampshire RG21 2XS
and London
Companies and representatives
throughout the world

Author: Anne Mountfield

Designed and typeset by The Pen and Ink Book Company Ltd, London

Illustrations by Jane Cheswright and Trevor Ricketts

Picture research by Faith Perkins

Printed in Hong Kong

British Library Cataloguing in Publication Data

Mountfield, Anne
    Looking back at houses and homes.–
    (Looking back at).
    1. Dwellings - History – Juvenile
    literature
    I. Title
    643'.09   TK303

ISBN 0-333-43940-6
ISBN 0-333-43946-5 Series

Photographic Credits

t=top b=bottom l=left r=right

The author and publishers wish to acknowledge, with thanks, the following photographic sources: 25r, 43t J Allan Cash, London; 31 BBC Hulton Picture Library, London; 21r, 37b, 42 (photograph John Bethell) Bridgeman Art Library, London; title page, The British Library, London; 7, 9, 13l, 17, 39l Douglas Dickins; contents page, 25l, 30-31, 32-33 Mary Evans Picture Library, London; 1 Fotocolor ENIT, Rome; 32b Fotocolor ESIT, Cagliari; 22 Fotomas Index; 5, 36 Sally and Richard Greenhill; 43b Robert Harding Photograph Library, London; 6r, 28, 40 Michael Holford; 10l, 14l, and r, 21l, 29, 34l, 39r Hutchison Photograph Library, London; 14 L Murray Robertson; 23l (photograph J Gibson), 26-27 (photograph John Bethell, 35 (photograph J Whittaker) National Trust Photograph Library, London; 20, 30 Picturepoint (UK); 18, 23r, 27 41 Ann Ronan; 10r Sheridan Photograph Library; 34-35 Frank Spooner Pictures; 6l, 8, 12, 28-29 Zefa (UK)

Cover illustration courtesy of The British Library, London

The publishers have made every effort to trace the copyright holders, but if they have inadvertently overlooked any, they will be pleased to make the necessary arrangement at the first opportunity.

Note to the reader
In this book there are some words in the text which are printed in **bold** type. This shows that the word is listed in the glossary on page 46. The glossary gives a brief explanation of words which may be new to you.

Contents

Introduction

We all need somewhere to live. We need a home. Homes are shelters. In cold countries, homes keep people warm and dry. In hot countries, they shade people from the Sun. People need a safe place to sleep. They also need somewhere to meet their family and friends, and to store the things they own. Our home is the place where we feel we belong.

Caves and shelters

The first people hunted for their food. They gathered plants and berries. They followed wild animals from place to place. They lived in caves, or in huts made of branches or grass. Sometimes, they dug holes in the ground, and covered them with grasses or skins. These shelters were used mostly for sleeping. Fires were lit outside, for cooking and for warmth. These fires would also frighten away wild animals.

Starting to build

About 7000 years ago, people learned how to grow crops. They began to keep animals in herds. They no longer needed to hunt. These people were the first farmers. The animals were their food. People began to live in groups and to share their work. In some places, the land did not grow enough food to feed everyone. People had to move on when their animals needed fresh grass. The people built huts, or made tents which could be moved easily. Sometimes, they put a fence around the huts and tents to keep everyone safe from attack. These settlements were called camps.

As people learned more about farming, they began to live in the same place. They did not need to move around. People started to build more solid houses. They made tools to help them build. They also learned how to use different materials. They divided their houses into rooms, and added new parts, like windows and chimneys.

◀ Lighting fires used to be hard work. Early people had to rub sticks together until they began to burn. Once a fire was burning, the people tried to keep it lit for a long time.

▼ People in ancient Britain lived in small huts of mud and sticks. Roofs were made from grass. The fences used to protect people from wild animals and from enemies.

Finding materials

The first builders used the materials for houses that they could find nearby. They could not carry heavy materials from other parts of the country. Houses were made of stone or wood. Bricks, made of clay, were also used. Stone and clay were taken from the ground near the buildings. Wood was cut from the forests. In some places, mud and leaves were used.

Today, builders use materials made in factories. These materials can be brought from all over the world very easily. This means that houses in different countries look more alike than they did in the past.

▼ Today, houses are built in large numbers. The same materials and designs can be seen in many parts of the world. These houses are in Detroit, in the United States. They are warm, dry and comfortable.

Places of safety

People first built homes to keep themselves safe. Danger came from the weather, wild animals and enemies. Homes were used for shelter and sleeping. People cooked, ate and worked outside their homes.

Keeping cool and warm

In cold countries, houses kept out the wind, rain and snow. Builders made thick walls and long, sloping roofs. In hot countries, houses needed to keep out the Sun. Some houses in Spain and Mexico were built into cliffs. The rock kept the houses cool. There were no windows or doors to let the Sun in. The entrance to the house was down a ladder from a hole in the roof.

▼ In desert areas, like Tunisia in North Africa, it is very hot. Underground houses like these stay cool and comfortable. They were made by people digging into the rock.

▲ Castles usually had a strong tower called the keep. The outer wall was called the curtain wall. This is Rochester Castle which was built in south east England in the 1100s. Its walls are four metres thick.

Keeping the enemy out

In the past, people burned fires at night. Fires kept them warm, and also kept wild animals away. People had to protect their own animals, too. They built a strong fence around their homes. They left one small opening in it. At night, they herded the animals inside the fence. Then, guards could defend the way into the village. Some people in Africa live in villages like this.

A hill is a safe place to live on. Enemies can be seen easily if they try to attack a village on a hill. Sometimes, the hill villages had a stone wall around them. These walled villages were called **hill-forts**.

Enemies tried to take over the hill-forts and villages. Sometimes, they won the fight. Then, they would live in the hill-fort until they were attacked, too.

Strong, walled **castles** were built as safe places for rulers to live in. Families, servants, and soldiers all lived there. If there was danger, the people who lived nearby could go into the castle for safety. They brought their animals, too! In Europe, between 1100 and 1500, whole towns were often built within castle walls. There were guards on the gates into the towns.

▼ In some countries, people have to build houses in very wet places. They may be close to marshy rivers or on land which floods easily. Stilts keep the homes above the water. These houses are on the Indonesian island of Sulawesi.

Floods and earthquakes

In some parts of the world, there is danger from floods and earthquakes. Floods wash away buildings. People and animals are often drowned if they cannot get away in time. Earthquakes shake the ground. Buildings may fall down and kill people. Houses have to be built in such a way that they remain safe.

Houses in Japan are in danger from earthquakes. They used to be built of paper and tall grass plants called **bamboo**. If they fell, they did not hurt people too much. Today, the Japanese build their houses on concrete blocks. The houses move as the ground moves. This means that fewer houses fall down in earthquakes.

On the move

Some people do not live in one place all the time. They travel around. They take their homes with them. These are called **mobile homes**. In the past, people travelled around in search of food and often lived in tents. In some parts of the world, people still live in mobile homes. Some live in tents or on boats. Others live in wagons. Today, mobile homes are often used by people on holiday.

Tents

People who travel around are called **nomads**. Some North American Indian peoples, such as the Sioux, Blackfoot and Cheyenne, were nomads. In the 1500s, they used to hunt and farm the lands near the Rocky Mountains. Spanish explorers brought horses to North and South America. Horses made it easier for people to hunt for food. Many of the Indian people gave up farming and became wandering hunters. They mainly hunted bison. They ate bison meat and used the skins for many things, including clothes and shoes. The hunters slept on fur rugs. They lived in cone-shaped tents called **tepees**. These were made from bison skins stretched over wooden poles. Since the hunters were often travelling, the tepees had to be light. When the hunters wanted to move on, they folded the skins and tied them to wooden frames. These frames, called **travois**, were dragged along by dogs or horses. There were no carts with wheels.

In many desert places, such as North Africa and the Middle East, nomadic people still travel with tents. The tents are often made from pressed animal hair called **felt**. The tents and their belongings are carried by camels.

▼ The Bedouin are Arab people, who live in the deserts of the Middle East. They travel across the desert to look for food for their flocks. They weave strips of cloth and sew them together. They use this cloth to make their tents.

Living on boats

Goods were often carried from place to place by river or canal. It was easier to move around on water than on land. The boats which carried the goods were called **barges**. Families lived on these barges. In Europe, some of these old boats are now holiday homes. Others, such as the barges on the Rhine River, are still homes. Canal boats used to be pulled along by horses. Today, they are driven by engines.

Wagons

In the 1800s, many people travelled across North America. They wanted to find new places to live. On the journey, their home was a wagon. The wagon was a cart with wooden hoops fixed over it. Cloth could be drawn over the hoops for shelter. These wagons looked like boats with sails. They were called 'prairie schooners'.

Travellers are some of the last nomads in Europe. They used to travel in painted caravans that were pulled by horses. Today, some have trailers pulled by cars and some travel in vans. Many travellers can no longer find anywhere to camp. In some countries, there are sites that are kept just for them.

▲ Hong Kong is an island. It is very crowded. Many people live in boats around the island. Many of the boats, or sampans, are decorated for the Chinese New Year. The large, colourful boat is a floating restaurant.

▲ The families who crossed North America used wagons like this. They took all their belongings in them. This made the wagons very heavy. They had to be drawn by large teams of horses or oxen.

Building houses

People used to build their own homes. They built them out of whatever materials they could find. They decided the shape and the size of their homes. In some places, this still happens. Families build their own homes. They build them in the same way that people have always done. The way of building houses has not changed for thousands of years.

In other places, styles of houses have changed. People used their homes differently. Perhaps they wanted bigger rooms, or they wanted to decorate their houses. People began to pay workers to help them to build their homes.

▼ People all over the world make homes from things they can easily find around them. These homes are made by the Dinka people in Sudan. They are made from grass held together by thin strips of wood from young trees.

Builders

Bricklaying, tiling and carpentry are all skills, or **crafts**. They were used in Egypt and Babylon thousands of years ago. The Romans developed new skills such as laying floors and bringing water to homes.

Workers often learned a single craft. In Europe, about 500 years ago, craft workers formed groups called **guilds**. In order to join the guild, young workers had to prove that they were good at their craft. These were skills like wood-carving, stone-carving and glass-making.

▼ Stonemasons carve stone. They have to use special stone to cut it to the shape the builders need. They often carve decorations on it. Today, stonemasons still work like these stonemasons in the 1500s.

▲ Andrea Palladio designed large villas, palaces and churches. This villa is in the town of Vicenza in Italy. Palladio used tall columns and statues to make his buildings look like those built in Roman times.

In the past, it took many skills and a long time to build a large house. Everything was done by hand. Today, the workers do not need to be so skilled. Windows, doors, sometimes even whole walls, are made in factories. They are brought to the building site ready-made. The builder fits them into place. Even a large house can be built quickly today.

Planning houses

Kings, queens and other rulers wanted large houses which looked beautiful. They wanted to show other people how important they were. The builders of these houses needed drawings to help them. The drawings showed all the building details. These drawings are called **plans**.

People who draw plans for the builders are called **architects**. They want to make buildings strong and beautiful. They often learn from each other. Andrea Palladio was an Italian architect in the 1500s. He studied the work of the Roman architect named Vitruvius. Palladio wanted his buildings to look like Roman buildings. Many other architects learned from Palladio.

Today, many architects work as part of a building team. They work with new materials like steel and **plate-glass**. They design whole blocks of flats or streets of houses.

What are houses made of?

People built houses out of whatever material they found nearby. In Papua New Guinea, it might be palm leaves and wood. In the deserts of the Middle East, it might be goatskin to make a tent. These materials last for a while but then they begin to rot.

Stone and brick last longer than grass or leaves. The stones and the bricks are heavy to carry. Today, many builders use new, lighter materials. They are easier to move around and they make strong buildings.

Mud and straw

Mud is easy to find and to use. Soil can be mixed with water to form a paste. The paste is left to dry out and harden. Houses were made in this way in ancient Egypt. In the Middle East, houses of several floors, or **storeys**, were built from mud. In Europe, some early cottages were built up from layers of mud and straw.

Leaves and wood

Leaves and grasses are easy to carry and to press into shape, but they catch fire easily. Reeds were woven into mats and used as roofs, walls and doors in places such as Peru in South America, and in South East Asia. In Africa, grass was often used in the building of a home. In forest areas, wood makes a cheap building material. People who went to live in North America and Australia often made log cabins from whole tree trunks. The bark protected the wood from rotting. In other places, wooden frames and flat planks of wood were used. Planks need to be painted, polished or varnished to protect them from the weather.

◀ The Pueblo Indians live in the south-west of the United States. Their traditional homes are made of a kind of clay called adobe. The windows are very small so that the sunlight cannot get in. The people build on new rooms every time they need more space.

Bricks

In hot, dry parts of the world, there are often not many trees. There is no wood for building. Bricks made out of clay are used. The clay dries quickly in the Sun. In colder countries, bricks have to be baked in ovens before they are hard enough to use. Then, they become strong and last a long time.

Stone

Stone is strong and also lasts a long time. It is cut, or **quarried**, out of rock. Then, the stone is shaped into blocks and carried to a building site. Different kinds of stone are often found in one country. Houses in each place were made from the stone that was nearby.

▲ These bricklayers are in Luxor in Egypt. People in Egypt have made bricks like these for thousands of years. The bricks are stuck together with a mud mixture called mortar.

▲ This house in the Philippines is made using many different materials. Wood, bamboo, leaves and rush matting have been used. These grow nearby and are cheap. The Philippine people have also used corrugated iron which has been made in another place.

Concrete and cement

Almost 2000 years ago, the architect Vitruvius described a rock powder which could be mixed with lime and stones. This mixture was so hard that it stayed set, even under water. Vitruvius called this rock powder 'cementum'. We call it cement. Concrete is made from a mixture of small stones, sand, water and cement powder. The mixture hardens very quickly.

Roofs and walls

Every house needs a roof. The shape of the roof depends on the climate. It also depends on the materials from which it is made.

Protection from the weather

In hot, dry countries, houses often have flat roofs. These keep the rooms below cool. Sometimes, stairs lead up to the roof. In the evenings, when the Sun has gone down, people like to sit and sleep there. Flat roofs have a very slight slope. If there is any rain, the water will drain away down the slope.

▼ The roofs of these Swiss houses are very steep. The snow is like a blanket on top of the roof. When the snow begins to melt, it runs off the roof easily. The roof overhangs the walls to keep the snow from blocking the windows and doors.

In wet countries, houses have steep roofs. The rain runs down the slope of the roof and is kept off the walls. Sometimes, it drains into water channels, called **gutters**. These channels collect the water from the roof. A drainpipe carries the water from the gutters to the ground.

Roofing materials

In countries such as Nepal and the United States, houses near forest areas use wooden tiles called **shingles** for their roofs. In other places, roofs are made of clay tiles or with blue-grey **slates**. Slate is a rock that splits easily into thin, flat pieces.

Some houses have roofs made of straw, reeds, turf or grass. These are called **thatched** roofs. They are warm in the winter and cool in the summer but they catch fire easily. After a while they rot and have to be replaced.

▲ Thatched roofs are found in many parts of the world. This house is in South Korea. Thatch is easy to make and is cheap. The straw, grass or reeds that are used can be easily found.

Today, roofing materials made in factories are often used. These last a long time and make roofs watertight.

Walls

The walls of a house have to be strong. They hold up the roof and any upper floors. Sometimes, walls are decorated. There may be stone carvings or patterns made out of brick, wood or stone. Sometimes, the walls are painted with bright colours.

▼ In Mauritania, in West Africa, the houses are made from clay. They are decorated with a traditional design. There are clay homes in other parts of Africa. These are also decorated, sometimes with bright colours and pictures.

In Europe, about 500 years ago, people began to hang cloths on their inside walls. These wall hangings were called **tapestries**. Some of them were pictures woven in thread. They showed people, animals and birds. The tapestries helped to keep the house warm. Inner walls were sometimes covered with carved panels of wood.

Wallpaper was first used in Asia, where it was hung on the walls, like posters. In the 1600s, people in Europe began to copy the designs used on Chinese wallpapers. The wallpapers were painted by hand. They were very costly. They were not pasted to the wall but were framed in long, wooden panels. Wallpaper has become cheaper in the last 100 years. It can now be printed in rolls by machines.

Doors and windows

The first houses had no doors. The entrance to the house was sometimes covered with skins or branches. When wooden doors were made, they were fixed to the door posts. A small flap of wood or metal, called a **hinge**, let the door move. It could be opened to let in light and air. It could be closed for warmth and safety.

Houses were often shared with animals. Doors were often made so that the top and bottom worked separately. They could be opened at the top to let in the light. The bottom half could be kept closed, to keep animals in or out.

Sometimes, doors needed to be very large, so that carts and horses could go through. The big doors were too heavy to open all the time. They often had small doors cut into them. These were called **wicket** gates.

The doors of palaces and rich people's houses were often very beautiful. Wooden doors were often carved with flowers or leaves. Sometimes, doors were made of a metal called **bronze**. The bronze was beaten with special tools so that the doors might have pictures on them of people or animals.

On some houses, doors were covered by roofs held up by pillars. These were called **porches**. Porches were very useful. People waiting in the rain or the hot Sun could take shelter under porches.

▼ Doors can be plain or decorated. Some doors are very large. They are used in castles or farms. Revolving doors are used where many people often go in and out. These doors cannot be left open.

decorated doorway of the **1800s**

wicket gate   stable door   revolving door

Windows

The first windows were just narrow slits in a wall. They let in a little light, but they kept the rain out. Very few windows had glass in them, because glass was very expensive. Wooden shutters or pieces of animal horn were used instead. Many houses still have wooden shutters. Window glass used to be made from blown glass. The bubble of glass was lifted away from the blowpipe by an iron tube. The tube left a blob in the glass. You can see these whirls in the middle of old glass window panes.

In the late 1700s, a new style of window was invented in Britain. These windows opened and closed by sliding up or down. They were called **sash windows**. They could be opened at the top or the bottom.

Glassmakers found out how to make bigger sheets of glass. Window panes became larger. Today, steel frames can hold up the roof or the upper storeys of a house. As a result, whole walls can be made into windows, using sheets of plate-glass.

▼ This house is in Rajasthan in India. Some of the windows have shutters. These block out the light. They block out the heat as well. The other windows are covered by a carved screen. This lets in air and some light through the fine holes.

▼ The first windows had no glass. This was a problem, because they let in cold air as well as light. Even when glass was invented, it was very costly. Glass was not made in large sheets, but in small panes.

North African window

early European window

sash window

Keeping houses safe

The first doors were closed with wooden bars called **latches**. The latch was fastened to the door. It was held by another piece of wood on the doorpost. People lifted the latch to open the door. Latches made it possible to keep out the wind and animals. They were easy to open, so they did not keep out thieves.

Another simple way to close a door is to use a **bolt**. A bolt is a sliding piece of wood or metal fixed to the door. It pushes into a hollow in the doorpost. A bolt on the inside can act as a lock. Doors cannot be locked from the outside with a bolt!

▲ These are locksmiths in the 1600s. They did all their work by hand. The keys and locks they made were very large and heavy. They were also quite easy to copy.

Locks

The earliest way of locking a door from the outside was used in Egypt, about 4000 years ago. A wooden bolt was made with three holes in it. When it was pushed into the lock, three pegs fell into the holes. The key to the lock had three pegs in it, too. When it was pushed under the bolt, it raised the three pegs.

About 2000 years ago, the Romans made metal locks. These locks used a different kind of key. Ridges on the key pushed a spring, which made a bolt fall into place. These **spring locks** were the first to have small keys that were easy to carry.

▲ A latch is the most simple way of keeping a door closed. Latches are used on doors that do not need to be locked. A bolt helps keep people out. It can only work on one side of a door. A padlock can lock the bolt so it cannot be moved.

Four hundred years ago, large iron locks were made in Europe. The keys were easy to copy, so the locks were not very safe. In Britain, in 1818, Jeremiah Chubb invented a new kind of lock. Each key had six or more small cuts, or notches, at the end. These were cut at different levels on each key. The key had to be an exact match before it would open the lock. The Chubb lock made houses much safer from thieves.

In 1861, Linus Yale invented a safer lock. The key has notches all along its edge. When it is pushed into a tube, it pushes up metal pins. The pins fit the key notches. This means the key can turn the tube to unlock the catch on the door.

Some locks have a dial. There are numbers on the dial. You have to move the dial around to the numbers in the right order. If you get the order wrong, the lock will not open. These **combination locks** are not new. Pictures of the same kind of lock have been found that are dated 1420! Combination locks are only used in houses if people want to keep something especially safe.

Today, many people also keep their homes safe with burglar alarms and hidden cameras. These warn the owner or the police if someone tries to break in.

Yale lock

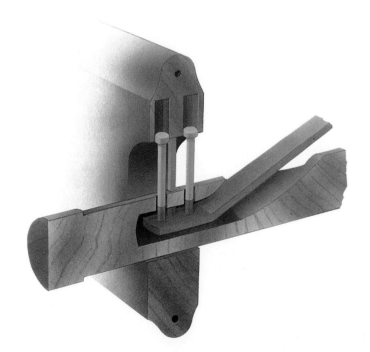

Egyptian locking bolt

▲ People tried several kinds of locks. They needed something strong and secure. They also needed something small and light. No one wanted to carry huge, heavy keys around with them.

Floors and ceilings

The simplest floors were made of earth which was beaten flat. Sometimes, they were covered with **rushes**, to make them warm. The rushes were replaced when they became dirty. Stone, brick and tile floors have also been used for hundreds of years. They are very useful in kitchens where the floor needs to be washed often.

In hot countries, marble floors stay cool. The Romans made patterned floors. They made pictures with coloured chips of marble. The chips were set in cement. These patterns are called **mosaics**.

In colder countries, floors were often covered with skins or rugs made out of rags. Carpets were very expensive indeed. In the 1800s, a cheap floor covering was made using linseed oil. This was called **linoleum** and it became very popular.

Carpets

Nomad peoples in the Middle East use carpets as furniture. They sit on them and sleep on them. When the nomads move on, they roll up their carpets and carry them along with their tents.

◀ The Romans made patterned mosaic floors for their villas. In the main rooms they made pictures like those in the centre of this floor. It took a long time to lay a mosaic floor. Clay tiles were quicker and cheaper to use. They are still popular in hot parts of the world.

Between the 1200s and the 1500s, the first carpets came by boat to Europe from China, India and Turkey. They had bright and colourful patterns. Only very rich people could buy them. At first, they were draped over chests and tables. They were too precious to walk on! They were also hung on the walls, like paintings, or used to cover beds.

By the 1700s, carpets were being made in Europe. Many towns such as Wilton, in Britain, have given their names to types of carpet. In the late 1700s, carpets began to be made in the United States. Making carpets in factories meant that they were much cheaper. More people could buy them.

▲ This ceiling was designed in the 1700s. The designer was a man named Robert Adam. The patterns are of flowers, fruit and leaves. They are moulded from plaster and then stuck on.

Ceilings

Early ceilings were also the floor of the room above. You could see all the wooden beams which held up the boards. Sometimes, the beams were carved or painted. In the 1500s and 1600s, the ceilings of important rooms in large houses were covered. A mixture of lime, sand and water was used. This mixture was called **plaster**. Often, there were shapes and patterns in the plaster. Some ceilings were made of smooth plaster. They were painted with pictures. Today, most ceilings are plastered. The beams, or supports, of the floor above cannot be seen.

▲ This boy is in Pakistan. He is weaving a traditional carpet. The first carpets brought to Europe were made in the same way. It takes a very long time to make a carpet by hand. There are many patterns made from dyed wool or cotton.

Stairs and lifts

In the first houses, everyone lived, ate and slept on the ground floor. There were no upper floors. The houses were often crowded. When people wanted more room, they built a platform above the ground. They used a ladder to climb up to it. The platform was a place to store things. Hay or bedding could be kept there.

When people found out how to build upper floors, they needed a safe way to reach them. They learned how to build stairs. Then, they could build much bigger houses. The houses could be several storeys high.

Stairs

Staircases take up a lot of space. The first staircases were often built outside houses. Sometimes, in bigger houses, the stairs were built inside a round tower. The stairs went around a central pillar. Stairs like this are called a **spiral** staircase. They were made from wood, stone or brick. Often, they were very steep and very dark.

In the 1500s, carpenters built sloping wooden staircases. They carved faces, flowers and plants on the bannister and on the posts. In the 1700s, large staircases were built out of marble. They were very grand. They made the owner of the house feel important.

Today, most staircases are very plain. They are not too steep, and are often covered with carpet.

◀ This outside staircase was built 600 years ago. It is being made of carved stone. The stonemasons are working at the bottom of the stairs. The finished stone is being winched to the top where there is scaffolding to help the builders.

After lifts were invented, even higher buildings were built. In places like New York in the United States, the buildings were so tall that they were called 'skyscrapers'. Some of them are over 100 storeys high. In some new skyscrapers, lifts with glass walls travel up and down on the outside of the building. The people using the lifts can enjoy the view outside.

▼ This lift was raised by a pole pushing from underneath. The lift could only go up a few storeys. When the pulley lift was invented, lifts could travel up many floors.

▲ There are carved wooden staircases like this one in many old houses. This staircase was built in 1701. It is in Hanbury Hall, near Worcester, in England.

Lifts

People have known how to make buildings several storeys high for a very long time. Old buildings of four or five storeys are found in many parts of the world. People who lived in tall buildings had many stairs to climb. They must have been very tired when they reached the top floor!

In 1852, Elisha Graves Otis invented a safe lift. This kind of lift could carry people to the top of any building.

Heating the home

Fire gives heat and light. It is also dangerous. It can destroy our homes and our woodlands. We do not know how people first learned to make fire. Perhaps they saw lightning strike a tree, or perhaps the Sun set dry grass on fire.

Wood fires heated homes for thousands of years. People cooked on fires. They also used fire to keep wild animals away. In the 1200s, Marco Polo, an Italian explorer, saw coal being burned in China. In Europe, wood and pressed earth, called **peat**, were burned. After the 1600s, more coal was burned by people in Europe.

▼ At first, there were no chimneys. People lit fires on the floor. Later, they built the fire near a wall. They built high walls on each side of the fire. The smoke went up between these walls. These were the beginnings of chimneys.

Chimneys

The first houses had no chimneys. The fire was built in the middle of the floor. From there, the smoke found its way out of a hole in the roof. Often, the rooms would be filled with smoke. The people and objects in the room would become filthy with smoke dust. This smoke dust is called soot.

When people built fireplaces, the smoke went up through a small chimney, called a **flue**. The flue was added on to the outside of the house. The first flues were wooden and were lined with clay. By the 1400s, chimneys were being built of brick or stone. They did not catch fire as easily as the wood and clay chimneys.

The soot made by coal smoke can block chimneys. In the 1800s, small boys worked as chimney sweeps. They crawled into the huge open fireplaces and up into the chimneys. From there, they brushed the soot down to the fireplace.

▼ Large houses often had very large chimneys. Several fireplaces opened out into one chimney. These chimneys became very sooty. Young boys climbed up the chimneys to clean them. It was a dangerous job.

Central heating

The Romans invented a kind of central heating. They built a closed fire, or **furnace**, below their houses. The hot air rose through the floors and behind the walls to an opening in the roof. Central heating was not used again for more than a thousand years.

The United States was one of the first countries to use central heating again. In 1877, a group of houses was heated from one central place. Pipes took the heat to the houses. In some parts of Russia, Denmark and Germany, this type of heating is used today.

Central heating came to Europe in the late 1800s. People found new ways of heating water and air. These systems can be run by oil, electricity or gas. The heat travels along pipes or through vents. We can choose when to turn the heating on or off. We can also choose how hot to make our homes. We set a timer to turn the heat on and off.

There is a new kind of heating, which uses the Sun's rays. It is called **solar heating**. Panels covered with glass are put on the roof to attract the Sun's rays. This heats the water that is running through the panels to a boiler. The boiler provides hot water and central heating for the house.

▲ This house is in New Mexico in the United States. It has been designed to use the Sun's rays. The roof catches heat from the Sun. This is used to heat water. The hot water heats the house.

Lighting the home

Before glass was used, windows were just small openings in the walls. Houses were very dark inside. People got up at sunrise and went to bed at sunset.

Lamps and candles

The first lamps were made from clay or stone. Vegetable oils or the fat of some animals were burned. These lamps did not smell very nice. Candles made from beeswax smell sweeter than oil lamps. Most people could not afford these candles. They made their own candles. They dipped rushes in fat and burned them. The rushes were a kind of **wick**. They kept the flame burning. Candles were used by most people until the mid-1800s. There was no other way to light a home or a place of work.

In Europe, in the 1700s, some of the bigger houses had beautiful hanging lamps. These lamps had a large metal frame with candle holders all around it. The big lamps held hundreds of candles. They were called **chandeliers**. Often, pieces of glass were hung all over the lamps. The candlelight made the glass sparkle. Chandeliers could be lowered from the ceiling on chains, so that people could light and put out the candles.

▼ Lighting used to come from small oil lamps or candles. These lights were not very bright. The first good lighting came from paraffin lamps in the 1800s. Then lighting by gas was invented. The best light was made by electricity.

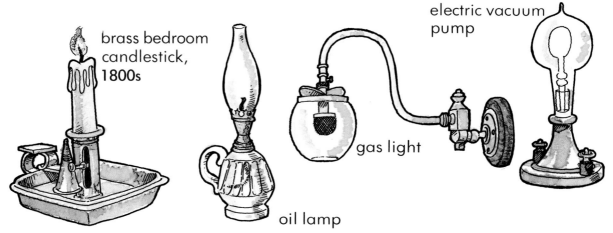

brass bedroom candlestick, 1800s

oil lamp

gas light

electric vacuum pump

◀ Chandeliers are usually hung with pieces of glass. The glass is cut at different angles. The candlelight is reflected by the glass. This makes the candlelight much brighter. Chandeliers must be kept clean to work well. They are difficult to clean and to light.

Gaslights and paraffin lamps

By the 1840s, some houses had gas lighting. It was not very bright. The lights flickered and were sooty. In 1859, oil was found in Pennsylvania in the United States. **Paraffin** was produced from oil. It was not expensive and gave a bright light. These paraffin lamps were not very safe. Paraffin is a liquid and it catches fire easily. If a lamp were knocked over, the whole house could be burned down.

The electric light bulb

In 1748, an important discovery was made. The American scientist, Benjamin Franklin, flew a kite in a storm. He saw that the metal on the kite attracted lightning. When it struck the metal there was a spark. Franklin knew that electricity caused this. The metal let electricity pass through it. No one knew how to store and use this light.

In the late 1870s, two men were working on ideas for electric lamps. In 1878, Joseph Swan made the first electric light bulb. In October, 1879, Thomas Alva Edison made a light bulb which glowed for 40 hours. Joseph Swan worked with an electrical current and metal rods. He put a thin rod into a glass bulb. The rod was made of **carbon**. Then, he took all the air out of the bulb. By the late 1880s, light bulbs were being made in the United States.

In the 1900s, homes began to be lit by electric light. At first, some people were afraid of electricity. They thought it could leak out from the light switch!

▼ Joseph Swan and Thomas Edison both worked to produce light bulbs. Swan was British. Edison was American. Their first light bulbs did not work very well.

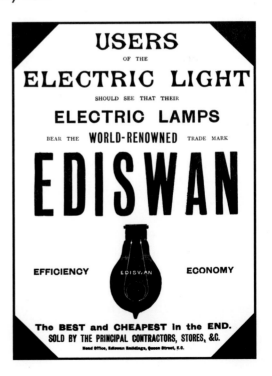

USERS OF THE ELECTRIC LIGHT SHOULD SEE THAT THEIR ELECTRIC LAMPS BEAR THE WORLD-RENOWNED TRADE MARK EDISWAN

EFFICIENCY EDISWAN ECONOMY

The BEST and CHEAPEST in the END.
SOLD BY THE PRINCIPAL CONTRACTORS, STORES, &C.
Head Office, Ediswan Buildings, Queen Street, E.C.

The water supply

If we had no water, we would soon die. Crops cannot grow without water. In places where there is no rain, people starve. In many parts of the world, clean water comes out of a tap. Dirty water goes down a drain. Yet, in other parts of the world, water has to be carried long distances. It comes from rivers, lakes and wells. When it rains, the water is collected and stored with care.

Wells and pumps

A **well** is a store of water below the ground. One old Chinese well was said to be nearly 500 m deep. Villages and towns grew up beside rivers or lakes, or near springs and wells. At first, the water was pulled up from the wells in buckets. Then, pumps were made. The water was pumped up by hand or machine. It was carried back to the home in buckets, or in water jugs. This was hard work. People soon tried to find a better way to bring water into their homes.

Storing water

About 3000 years ago, in the cities of Jordan, people built water tunnels. These were called **conduits**. They carried water into the cities from rivers and lakes. Each house had its own tank for water. This water tank was called a **cistern**. The cistern stored the water that flowed in from the conduits.

▼ This water cistern is in the remains of the city of Carthage, in North Africa. The Romans used cisterns like this to store water which came from mountains many miles away.

Water courses

Water cannot flow uphill, so water tunnels did not work in hilly country. The Romans solved this problem 2000 years ago. They built special bridges, called **aqueducts**. These carried the water channels high across the valleys.

The Romans ruled over many parts of Europe. Wherever they lived, they built water pipes and pumps. These brought water to public fountains and baths. When the Roman Empire came to an end, 1500 years ago, the water systems fell into ruins.

▼ The Romans made sure their cities had good water supplies. This aqueduct is in France, but it was built by the Romans. The water ran along a channel on the top.

Today's water

Today, many people have hot and cold water tanks in their homes. Other people still collect water from a river or well. The weather can cause many problems. In very hot countries, the rivers and wells will sometimes dry up during the dry season. In cold countries, the water in lakes freezes. Even the water in pipes can freeze, too. Since we all need water to stay alive, these problems have to be solved.

▼ There are still many people in the world who do not have water in their home. They have to fetch water from a public tap, a well or a river. This woman in India is carrying water home in the pots on her head.

Pipes and drains

Some people in the past knew that houses needed a supply of clean water. They also knew how to get rid of dirty water and waste matter. In the Indus valley of Pakistan, 5000 years ago, there were brick houses with drains. These drains carried away the dirty water. In Rome, the lavatories were joined to pipes under the ground, called sewers. The sewers were kept flushed by running water. This carried waste, or **sewage**, outside the city. Later, all this knowledge was forgotten.

▲ This sketch was from a newspaper in the 1850s. It was drawn to show the terrible slums of London. Houses were crowded and dirty. There was no clean water or proper drainage. There were many diseases. Doctors and other people fought for proper drainage and clean water.

▲ The channels in the ground are drains. They were built 5000 years ago in the city of Mohenjo-Daro in Pakistan. The city had a proper drainage system. Closed pipes came from the houses to these open channels. The channels were cleaned to keep them clear.

Four hundred years ago, in most cities in Europe, houses did not have clean water. Water was brought from rivers and lakes to the street pumps. This water was often dirty since the pipes were open to the air. Water carriers sold fresh spring water in the streets. Spring water was cleaner, but there were no lids on the buckets so dirt got into the water. There were no drains under the ground. There were only gutters to carry dirty water away. Gutters were at the side of, or down the middle of, the streets. Dirty water and waste were often thrown from windows into the street below. Many towns in the world still have drains above ground like this.

Dirty water and disease

Many people left the countryside to find work in the cities. The cities became very crowded. Lavatories often emptied into pools, called **cesspits**, under the houses. The water in wells and rivers was made dirty by sewage leaking from the cesspits. People died of diseases such as **cholera** and **typhoid fever**. They did not know how they caught these diseases.

By the 1800s, some doctors found out that very small living creatures, called **germs**, cause disease. The cholera and typhoid germs lived in dirty water. The water had been infected by waste. People then used the dirty water for drinking or cooking. In this way, killer diseases were easily spread. More and more people died. It was clear that something had to be done.

Sewage systems

In the 1800s, systems of underground sewers were built in Europe and the United States. Roads were dug up and underground tunnels were built. Drain pipes were then connected to the houses. People said the costs were too high, but fewer people died from diseases. Today, cities all over the world have underground sewers. There are still many places where there are no proper drainpipes to carry sewage away.

▼ In the 1870s, large underground sewers were built to carry away the waste and dirty water. They are still used today.

Kitchens

A place for cooking food has always been important. Sometimes, the kitchen was in a separate building. This was usually for safety in case of fire. In small houses, the kitchen was often the only warm room. It was used for living in, eating in and sleeping in.

Most cooking was done in the fireplace. A large pot, or **cauldron**, was used to boil food. It hung over the fire on metal chains. Soup, stew, or porridge, was cooked in it. Meat was roasted over the fire. A metal pole, called a **spit**, was stuck through the meat. The spit rested on a frame just above the flames. It could be turned from the side, so that the meat cooked all over. Brick ovens were built in the walls or chimney, near the fire. These were used for baking bread.

Cooking stoves

In the 1700s and 1800s, many kitchen fires burned coal instead of wood. Metal fireplaces, called **ranges**, were built. These had iron ovens and plates to stand pots and pans on. Ranges were polished with a paste called **blacklead**.

The first gas ovens were used in the 1870s. These new cookers did not work very well. Sometimes, there was not enough gas and the flames went out. Today, gas, electric and microwave cookers are used. They are easy to use and quick to clean.

▲ This is a kitchen in France in the 1800s. It has a large range. Part of the range held hot water. The water came out of the taps at the side. On the walls are all the pots and tools used for cooking.

▲ The first ovens were mainly for baking bread. Many people had no ovens. They took their pies and stews to the baker's oven. He would put them in his oven after he had baked the bread.

Washing clothes

Washing is not always done in the kitchen. Sometimes, it is done outside in rivers or lakes. In some places, a special room is used for washing. It is best to have hot water. During the 1800s, water was heated in a tub on the fire or range. The clothes were washed by thumping a wooden **dolly** up and down in the hot water. A dolly looked like a three-legged stool with a long-handled pole stuck through its centre. The water was squeezed out of the clothes by the rollers of a **mangle**. In 1907, an American, Alva J. Fisher, made a washing machine. This had an electric motor. The motor moved a dolly up and down in the water.

Storing food

Food that is kept too long goes bad. If we eat bad food, we will be ill. In the past, it was difficult to keep food for long. People tried to keep their food cool. Sometimes, meat was kept in a net-covered frame. This was called a **meat safe**. The safe let air cool the food but kept flies away. Cupboards, called **larders**, were often built in the coolest part of the house. There were air-holes in the wall. They let in fresh air.

The first machine which chilled air was invented in 1834. In this way, food could be kept fresh for days. The machine was called a **refrigerator**. It was invented in the United States by Jacob Perkins. In the 1920s, another American, Clarence Birdseye, found a way to freeze food. Today, many kitchens have freezers. Food can be stored in them for months.

▶ The first washing machines looked like this. The washing was done in the tub. The handle moved the water and the clothes around. The mangle was used to wring out the clothes.

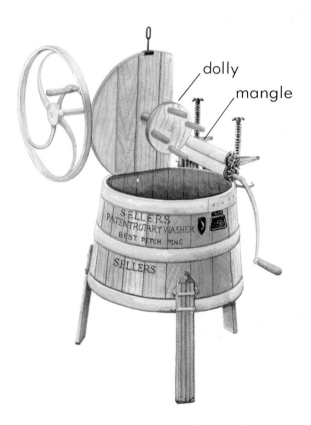

dolly

mangle

Dining rooms

About 1000 years ago, groups of people often ate their meals together. They sat at a long table in a room called a great hall. Tables were used only for meals. When the meal was finished, the wooden board was lifted off its legs, or **trestle**. It was then propped up against the wall.

In their own homes, most people ate in the room where they lived. Then, rich families began to have one room just for eating. Dining rooms were for special occasions.

Table manners

Between the 1100s and the 1500s, if you were about nine or ten, you would have started your first job. You might have been sent to live with a rich family. You would be a maid or a page. You would have to learn good table manners. You could not throw meat or fish bones under the table! You ate with your fingers. Everybody had a large piece of bread to eat with their meals. They broke off lumps of the bread to dip into the sauce or the gravy. The bread was also used to scoop food out of the bowl. Knives were used for cutting very tough food. Forks were not used until the 1500s.

▲ These people are in Japan. They are eating in a traditional way. They are kneeling at a very low table. The food is served in small bowls. Much of the food is eaten raw. People eat with chopsticks.

▶ People all over the world enjoy eating outside. These men and boys are in Saudi Arabia. They are sitting on a carpet, and eating spiced food from one large bowl. They eat using their right hands only.

Salt

Salt was very ~ecious. In the days before refrigerators, covering meat with salt was the only way to keep it from going bad. A large pot, or **salt-cellar**, stood in the middle of every table. If the family was rich, the salt-cellar was made of silver or gold. Important people sat at the top end of the table. This was above the large salt-cellar. The less important people sat at the bottom end of the table below the salt-cellar.

▶ In houses where important people lived there was usually a dining hall with a large table. This one is made from carved oak. It is long, so that many people can sit at it. People often sat on benches rather than chairs.

Tables and chairs

Kitchen furniture was plain and simple. It was made by local carpenters. They used strong wood such as oak, elm or yew. Dining room furniture was for guests to see and admire. The wood was often carved and polished. In the 1500s, in Europe, it was made from oak. By the 1800s, South American woods were also used. People liked light furniture. It could be finely carved. Tables and chairs were made from woods such as walnut, maple or rosewood.

The dumb waiter

In the 1800s, the kitchen was often in the basement of large homes. It took a long time to carry food from the kitchen to the dining room. Sometimes, houses had a small lift worked by hand. This was called a dumb waiter. The food was pulled up to the dining room on the dumb waiter by a servant.

Living rooms

Until about 200 years ago, people lived and worked in one room. This was used for cooking and might have to be shared with animals. Very few families had separate rooms where they could sit and relax in comfort. In hot countries, like Greece and India, there was often a shady inner courtyard. People could sit there in the evenings.

▼ Homes in China are often small. They have only a few rooms. The family cook, eat and sit in the living room. They keep many of their belongings there too.

Cushions and seats

The first seating was very simple. People sat on animal furs, or brushwood, or just on stones or logs. In Asia, carpets and cushions were used to sit on. In many old paintings, you can see Indian rulers sitting on heaps of silk cushions. Other people had to sit on the floor.

In Europe, chairs were first made from wood or stone. They were draped with rugs or furs. Living rooms in most houses were furnished only with tables and hard chairs.

Towards the end of the 1700s, chairs and sofas were made with padded seats and arms. This was called **upholstery**. All the work was done by hand. In the late 1800s, factories began using machines to make wooden furniture. It was less expensive, so more people could buy it.

The first sitting rooms

Rulers or rich people have houses with many rooms. Large Greek and Roman houses had rooms where the family and their friends could sit and talk. The rooms were often built to face south, so that they would be sunny in winter-time.

In Europe, some of the first sitting rooms were upstairs. They were built to catch the sunshine. These rooms were called **solars**. They were used by the family. Sometimes, a second room was built upstairs, where the women could sit while sewing and talking. This was called the **parlour**.

Town houses were built with upper storeys. The top floor was often made into a long **gallery**. Here, people could walk on rainy days. They could entertain their friends.

Drawing rooms

After 1700, people in many countries had furnished rooms where they sat after dinner. They drank tea, and talked with friends. These were called **withdrawing rooms**. Later, they were just called drawing rooms. In the largest and grandest houses, they were sometimes called the **salon**.

By the end of the 1800s, more families could afford to have a living room. This was often a show-piece, for friends to admire. It was only used on Sundays and for special occasions.

▲ The long gallery was often used during bad weather. The children played and had lessons there. People talked and read by the fireplace, or walked for exercise. Music and dancing also took place in the gallery.

▼ This is a drawing room in the 1870s. It belonged to the Hatch family. The curtains are heavy and shut out the sunlight. The room is crowded with dark furniture. All this was in fashion at that time.

Bedrooms

For thousands of years, most people slept on the floor. Others slept on platforms around the edges of a room. People did not have separate rooms for sleeping.

In some hot countries, people have always slept in **hammocks**. These are made from cloth or woven leaves. Hammocks can be tied up between two trees or two posts. They are light and easy to carry.

Beds

Thousands of years ago, the Egyptians had beds that were the same shape as the beds of today. The Greeks and Romans had couches. They used 'day-beds' for lying on at a feast or banquet.

For a long time, only rich people had beds. Most people had no special bedroom. Beds were kept on a raised platform at one end of the hall. There were curtains around the bed called hangings. These hangings kept out the draughts of cold air.

In some parts of Europe, country people slept on straw or on mattresses filled with leaves or feathers. Beds in cottages were very simple. They were like cupboards in the wall. They had doors that closed over them in the daytime.

By the 1500s, the **four-poster bed** was popular. It had curtains all around it. A four-poster bed seemed private even though other people shared the room. Children and servants often slept in the same room as the house owner. Their beds were like drawers on wheels. They could be tucked under the big bed during the day. These beds were called **truckle beds**.

Eyptian bed, 2690 BC

▲ Beds have not changed much over the years. Beds in ancient Egypt looked like beds today. Some beds in the past were very large. Several people could sleep in them.

large bed from an inn

◀ A futon is used in Japan. It is a thick cotton mattress on the floor. The pillow is supported by a separate woven frame and the bed is covered by a warm quilt. Japanese homes are very small. People fold futon beds away during the day.

▼ This Chinese bed has a hard base covered with a woven rush mat. The bed has curtains which completely cover it. They are drawn together at night to keep out any insects.

In the 1800s, the curtains around the bed were no longer needed. Houses were better built. There was not so much cold air around. Many people had separate rooms to sleep in. Then, coiled wire springs were put under the bed mattress. These made the beds more comfortable.

Bed coverings

People used many different covers for their beds. At first, animal skins or furs were used. In Europe about 500 years ago, some people started to use sheets and pillow cases for their beds. These were often made from a cloth called **linen**. In some places, feathers were stuffed into large cloth bags to make a warm bed covering, or quilt. Blankets were made of woven wool and they were often made at home.

Bedspreads and quilts were made of padded cotton, linen or silk. Sometimes, they were made from **patchwork**. The designs were often of birds, flowers and animals. Patchwork quilts were made in many countries. Some very fine quilts were made in New England in the United States. A young woman might make up to 14 quilts before she got married! The patterns on the quilts were to bring happiness and good luck.

Bathrooms and lavatories

Until the 1900s, very few houses had baths and bathrooms. Most people washed in a bowl or bath tub. When they wanted to take a bath, they had to fill a tub from jugs of hot water. Lavatories were often out of doors in backyards.

▼ The Roman baths at Bath in Britain, were built where hot springs come out of the ground. After the Romans, the baths were not used for a very long time. They became popular again in the 1700s.

Baths

In ancient Greece and Rome, people washed themselves very often. Their cities had public lavatories and baths.They had flushing water and sewers. These public baths were like a health centre today. There was a gym, a sauna and a swimming pool all in one building. People met there. They washed in warm water and sat in hot, steamy rooms. They exercised, and they discussed business. Then, they cooled off with a plunge into a cold pool of water. Going to the baths was a social occasion.

People began to think that public bathing was unhealthy. Public baths were no longer used. People washed in their own homes.

Early bath tubs came in all shapes and sizes. The 'slipper' bath looked exactly like a large slipper. A flap lifted so that a person could get in. The baths had to be filled with water by hand. In the 1850s, people heated the cold water in a bath by lighting a gas fire underneath it. The first piped hot water was stored in a tank that could keep it warm. This must have seemed a very great luxury.

Lavatories

The Romans built public lavatories. The next lavatories, that we know about, were in castles. They were called 'garderobes'. They were built in an outer wall. The waste fell down a hole, to the ground below.

In the 1500s, Sir John Harrington invented a way of removing waste matter. Water flowed from a tank to a **water-closet**. It flushed away waste. Queen Elizabeth I had one in her palace at Richmond in England.

Most people did not have water-closets. They used pots and chairs with the pots hidden under the seat. The seat lifted up like a lid. These chairs were called **commodes**. If you could afford it, you paid the 'night-soil' man to take your sewage away. If not, the refuse and sewage piled up in the gutters and courtyards. This spread disease.

hip bath

▲ In the past, there were no hot-water taps. Water had to be heated and carried to the bath. This means it was best to share baths, or have small ones. Hip baths and slipper baths were smaller than the baths we use today.

▲ This is a water-closet or lavatory made in 1887. Water was held in the tank above the pedestal. People pulled the chain to make it flush. The water and waste went out through a pipe.

41

Gardens

Long ago, the Egyptians made walled gardens. They grew fig trees and grape vines, vegetables and flowers. They made pools beside the Nile River. Blue lotus flowers grew in them.

Two thousand years ago, there were gardens in the walls of Babylon. The king of Babylon, Nebuchadnezzar, built the gardens for his wife. The gardens were in steps or **terraces**. They were said to be one of the wonders of the world. They were called the Hanging Gardens of Babylon.

Greek and Roman houses often had inner courtyards. People could sit there and enjoy the shade. There was a fountain in the middle of the courtyard. There were statues and pots of flowers.

Plants for gardens

In the 1200s, Marco Polo visited China. There, he saw gardens which were full of beautiful flowers. Many of these flowers, such as lilies and peonies, were not brought to Europe until the 1700s.

Green plants, called **herbs**, are grown to flavour food and to make medicines. In the 1500s, herbs were planted in patterns. Little hedges divided up groups of plants. This was called a **knot-garden**. Many people still use herbs in cooking. Some people know how to make medicines from herbs.

▼ These gardens are at Powys Castle in Wales. They are built at different levels to make terraces. Many plants are grown against or over the walls like the Hanging Gardens of ancient Babylon. Statues and paths were used to make the garden more interesting.

Sheltered gardens

Courtyard gardens were common in hot, dry countries. The walls gave shade from the Sun and the wind. These courtyards often had a fountain or a pool of water. The Chinese built gardens with walls on all sides. They were quiet places where people could think. Some of these gardens were made a long time ago. The gardens of Suchow can still be seen today.

In Japan, gardens were made around temples. Some temple gardens were made in the 1100s. They still exist. Some have many types of moss plants. Others are made up of small stones.

Cottage gardens

In Europe, country people grew fruit and vegetables near their homes. Sometimes, flowers were grown amongst the fruit and vegetables. Garden pests liked to eat the flowers better than the food plants. This mixing of plants is called 'cottage-style' gardening.

The English garden

For many years in Europe, gardens were made to a strict pattern. They had paved paths around neat flower beds. In the 1700s, there was a new style of garden. The big gardens around country homes were planted to look like natural countryside. Grass lawns, trees and shrubs were planted. These made a fine view from the window of the house.

▲ This garden is in Granada, in Spain. Spain was once ruled by Arab people from North Africa. The Arabs built many fine palaces and gardens. Small canals often ran through the middle of the gardens. Walled gardens are still built in hot countries today.

▲ Country people often grew their own food. They grew fruit and vegetables to last through the winter. They also grew flowers, because they looked pretty. The gardens were very simple. Cottage gardens like these are found in many parts of Britain today.

Quiz

How much can you remember? Try to do the quiz and use your glossary and index to help you check your answers.

1. Here are some types of beds with the letters mixed up. Try to find the correct words.
   a) UHOCC b) KOMAMCH, c) TLECRUK, d) ROFURESTOP

2. Where
   a) did people live in tepees?
   b) was the sash window invented?
   c) was wallpaper first used?
   d) was the earliest lock used?
   e) was central heating first used?

3. Match the description given in (a) to (f) with the words numbered (1) to (6) below them.
   a) a roof made of straw, reeds, turf or grass
   b) a very tall building
   c) a small gate set in a bigger one
   d) used to squeeze water from wet clothes
   e) a person who designs and plans houses
   f) a large lamp lit by candles.

   1) skyscraper
   2) chandelier
   3) mangle
   4) architect
   5) thatch
   6) wicket

4. Who
   a) made the first refrigerator?
   b) studied Roman buildings and became a famous architect?

c) invented the lock with the notched key?
d) invented the safety lift?

5. What
   a) are porches?
   b) are combination locks?
   c) is linoleum?
   d) is a flue?
   e) are hammocks?

6. Complete the following sentences with (a), (b), (c) or (d):
   1) People who travel in search of food are called
      a) landers.
      b) sweeps.
      c) nomads.
      d) commodes.

   2) Woven cloth pictures hung on walls are called
      a) posters.
      b) thermostats.
      c) tapestries.
      d) table-cloths.

   3) A metal pole used for roasting meat is called a
      a) peat.
      b) spiral.
      c) lead.
      d) spit.

   4) Roman floors made from small pieces of marble are called
      a) mosaics.
      b) cauldrons.
      c) solars.
      d) quilts.

   5) Travois are
      a) kings in Europe.
      b) wooden frames dragged by horses or dogs.

c) building skills.
d) carts drawn by horses.

6) Guilds are
a) a type of money used in Holland.
b) water plants used for building.
c) blocks of flats.
d) groups of craft workers.

7. Are these statements true or false?
a) Cement stays hard under water.
b) Slipper baths were shaped like slippers.
c) Between the 1300s and 1500s, the first carpets came to Europe from North America.
d) A meat safe is where butchers keep their money.
e) Knives were used long before forks.

8. Put the following events in the order they took place.
a) In Europe, towns were built with walls around the outside.
b) Carpet-making began in the United States.
c) People learned to grow crops and keep animals in herds.
d) Whole walls were made of plate-glass.
e) People in Europe began to copy designs used on Chinese wallpaper.

9. Which is the odd one out? Why?
a) slate, shingle, quarry, straw
b) tent, wagon, canal, barge
c) wood, coal, flue, peat,
d) aqueduct, jug, cauldron, trestle,
e) parlour, salon, shingles, solar

10. Here are ten words written backwards. Which five are names of types of building materials?

a) ESAESID, b) OOBMAB, c) SDAMON,
d) NIKS, e) ENOTS, f) STRESED,
g) RUOLRAP, h) DUM, i) SKCIRB,
j) SNEVO

Answers

1. a) COUCH, b) HAMMOCK, c) TRUCKLE, d) FOUR POSTER
2. a) North America, b) Britain, c) China, d) Egypt, e) Rome
3. (a) 5, (b) 1, (c) 6, (d) 3, (e) 4, (f) 2
4. a) Jacob Perkins
b) Andrea Palladio
c) Jeremiah Chubb
d) Elisha Graves Otis
5. a) roofs held up by pillars which covered doors
b) locks which could be opened at certain times by the right series of numbers
c) a floor

6. (1) c, (2) c, (3) d, (4) a, (5) b, (6) d
7. a) true, b) true, c) false, d) false, e) true
8. (c), (a), (e), (b), (d)
9. a) quarry (all the others are roofing materials)
b) canal (all the others are mobile homes)
c) flue (all the others can be burned)
d) trestle (all the others can hold water)
e) shingles (all the others are types of living rooms)
10. b) BAMBOO, d) SKIN, e) STONE, h) MUD, i) BRICKS

45

Glossary

aqueduct: a pipe or channel built to carry water across a valley or through a tunnel
architect: a person who designs buildings and draws the plans for builders to follow

bamboo: a very tall type of grass with a hard hollow stem. Bamboo can grow up to 40 m high. It is found in warm climates
barge: a wide flat-bottomed boat. Barges are used for carrying goods
blacklead: a black mineral called plumbago. It can be used for polishing metal or making pencils
bolt: a bar made of wood or metal which slides across the door and frame to fasten the door shut
bronze: a metal made of copper and tin

carbon: an important chemical found in fuels, foods and all living things on earth
castle: a large walled fort. A nobleman lived there with his family and soldiers to fight off enemies
cauldron: a large kettle or pot for boiling in. It is hung over a fire
cesspit: a large underground hole which is used to collect waste drainage from a house
chandelier: a large frame with branches for holding lights. It hangs from the ceiling
cholera: a disease which gives people very bad diarrhorea and vomiting. Cholera is spread by unclean water and food, and it is easily caught
cistern: a tank or reservoir for holding water
combination lock: a type of lock which uses several connected actions or numbers instead of a key. The correct actions must be followed in the right order before the lock can be opened
commode: a chair with a deep seat which holds a chamber pot. The pot is hidden under a lid
conduit: a pipe or channel that carries water or other liquid
craft: work that needs skill and must be studied and learned. Carpentry is a craft

dolly: a wooden stick with arms at one end used for stirring clothes in a washing tub

felt: a kind of thick cloth made by pressing hair or wool flat

flue: a pipe which carries hot air, smoke or gases to the outside of a building
four-poster bed: a large bed with four upright posts at each corner. Curtains are often hung between these posts. They are drawn around the bed at night
furnace: a closed chamber in which things can be heated to a very high temperature

gallery: a covered walkway or passage. Galleries are often built above ground level and open at one side to overlook a room below
germ: a tiny living thing that can cause diseases. Germs can only be seen with a very strong microscope
guild: a society set up to help and support groups of workers with similar skills
gutter: a channel or drain at the edge of a roof or side of a street. A gutter carries off rain water

hammock: a cloth or net hung by cords at each end. It is used as a bed
herb: any plant used for medicine or to add flavour in cooking
hill-fort: a group of buildings which have a strong wall around them and are on raised ground or a hill-top. This made it easier for people to defend themselves
hinge: a joint which allows one thing to swing on another

knot-garden: a patch of garden divided by stones or hedges where different herbs can grow

larder: a small room or cupboard where food can be kept cool and fresh
latch: a bar which fastens a door or gate shut. A latch is attached at one end, and the free end is lifted by a lever or handle
linen: a fine, smooth cloth made from flax
linoleum: a strong floor covering, made by treating a fabric with a linseed oil, resins and cork

mangle: a machine with two rollers used for pressing and draining off water from clothes
meat safe: a container for storing meat. The safe has fine air holes to protect the meat from flies
mobile home: any form of shelter which can be easily moved about
mosaic: a pattern, design, or picture which is made by fitting together many small pieces

nomad: someone who moves from place to place in search of food or to find grassland for animals. Nomads do not make their homes in one place

paraffin: a waxy liquid made from oil. It was used as a fuel

parlour: a small sitting room. It was usually simply furnished and private

patchwork: small pieces of fabric sewn together to make an attractive pattern of different colours.

peat: partly rotted plants in wet marsh land. Peat is soft and spongy to touch, but it can be dried out and used as a fuel

plan: a drawing to show the shape of something such as a building, as seen from above

plaster: a mixture of lime and sand made into a paste with water. It is used to coat walls or ceilings. It goes hard and feels smooth to touch

plate-glass: strong glass which is made in large sheets. Plate-glass is often used for large mirrors and windows in shops and offices

porch: the part of a building which covers or protects the outer doorway

quarry: a place where rocks are cut or dug from the ground

range: a large flat-topped kitchen stove. It is made of metal and contains a fire which heats the oven and hot plates

refrigerator: a cupboard-like machine which keeps air at a low temperature

rush: tall grass-like plant with slim, strong stalks. It grows in wet places

salon: a large room found in big houses where people can gather to sit and talk

salt-cellar: a container that holds salt for use on the table

sash window: a sliding frame which holds window glass. It is balanced by weights which allow movement up and down

sewage: the waste matter which is carried away by water from buildings

shingle: wooden slabs used as a roofing tile

solar: a room positioned so that it catches a lot of sunlight

solar heating: a way of using energy from the Sun's rays to heat water for heating houses

spiral: a shape or line that curves round and round while moving away from a point

spit: a pointed stick on whch food can be stuck and then held over flames to be cooked

spring lock: a door fastening which contains a spring that is released when touched by a key

storey: the part of a building which is on the same level or floor. Some buildings have several storeys or floors built one on top of the other

tapestry: a fabric in which coloured threads are stitched to form pictures or patterns. Tapestries covered walls and furniture

tepee: a North American Indian's tent made from skins or cloth. It is stretched over a frame of poles

terrace: a flat piece of ground cut into a slope, like a large step

thatch: a thick and waterproof roof covering made from layers of straw, rushes or palm-leaves

thermostat: an electronic device for keeping temperature steady

travellers: groups of people who prefer to travel around, rather than settle down in one spot

travois: a pair of trailing poles attached to each side of a horse's saddle. They are joined by a piece of cloth and carry people and belongings

trestle: a wooden or metal criss-cross framework that supports a flat surface such as a table

truckle bed: a servant's or child's bed on low wheels which could be pushed under a larger bed

typhoid fever: a serious disease which causes a high temperature, red spots and stomach pains. It is spread by unclean food and water

upholstery: the springs, padding, stuffing and covers which are fitted over a frame. Upholstery makes chairs and sofas more comfortable

water-closet: a lavatory where the waste is carried off by water to a drain

wick: the twisted threads of cotton or other substance which draws up oil or grease to the flame of a candle or lamp

wicket: a small door in or near a larger gate

withdrawing room: a comfortably furnished sitting room. In the past, people used to meet there after their meal

Index